Navigating The Canadian Real Estate:

Complete Guide

Kyla Lovell

Navigating The Canadian Real Estate: Complete Guide

Copyright © 2024 by Kyla Lovell

All rights reserved. No part of this publication may be reproduced, distributed, or transmitted in any form or by any means, including photocopying, recording, or other electronic or mechanical methods, without the prior written permission of the author, except in the case of brief quotations embodied in critical reviews and certain other non-commercial uses permitted by copyright law. For permission requests, write to the author through this email: ibc@pbbankers.com.

ISBN: 9781738225118

Disclaimer:

The information in this book is true and complete to the best of the author's knowledge. All recommendations are made without guarantee on the part of the author. The author disclaims any liability in connection with the use of this information.

Contents

Introduction 5
1 — The Canadian Advantage 6
   An Overview of the Canadian Real Estate Market 6
   Why Invest in the Canadian Real Estate? 7
2 — Establishing a Solid Foundation 10
   Mindset Shift 10
   Enhancing Financial Literacy 10
   Goal Setting 12
      1.   Define Your Vision 12
      2.   Set Specific Goals 12
      3.   Take Massive Action 13
      4.   Review and Adjust 13
3— An Overview Canadian Real Estate Market 14
   Research Market Demographics and Trends 14
      1.   Market Trends Analysis 14
      2.   Demographic Considerations 14
      3.   Researching Local Amenities 14
   Mortgage Options and Financing Strategies 15
   Due Diligence and Risk Management 16
4— Taking Advantage of Leverage 18
   Proper Utilization of Finances 18
   Mortgage Strategies 19
   Using Other People's Money to Build Wealth 20

5— Financing Options 23
  Traditional Mortgage Financing 23
  Home Equity Line of Credit (HELOC) 24
  Private Financing 25
  Taking Advantage of Government Programs and Incentives 26
  Creative Financing Strategies 27
6 — Building Your Real Estate Portfolio 29
  Setting Investment Goals 29
  Capitalization and Financing 30
  Establishing a Diversified Real Estate Portfolio 30
  Managing and Optimizing Your Portfolio 32
7— Optimizing Your Cash Flow 34
  Implementing Efficient Property Management Techniques 34
  Minimizing Tenant Turnover and Vacancy 36
8— Legacy Planning and Long-Term Wealth 38
  Preserving Wealth through Real Estate 38
  Tax Strategies for Canadian Real Estate Investors 39
  Wealth Transfer and Estate Planning 40
Conclusion 42

Introduction

This guidebook will offer you a thorough understanding of the potential in the Canadian real estate market, which can lead you to financial success. New and seasoned investors will find this book valuable since it contains skills, insights, and insights needed to navigate Canadian real estate.

The Canadian real estate sector presents many possibilities due to its encouraging government policies, stable economy, and solid property market. This book will help you to navigate the market's complexity and make informed choices.

You will cultivate a wealth-building attitude influenced by the likes of Robert Kiyosaki and Grant Cardone. A significant emphasis will be on financial literacy, including ideas like cash flow, risk management, and leverage. We'll highlight various funding alternatives, such as private financing and non-conventional approaches.

You will develop proficiency in deal evaluation and market analysis to help you spot profitable prospects. You will learn how to efficiently manage properties, grow your portfolio, and maximize cash flow. We'll also discuss long-term wealth and legacy planning, including wealth preservation, tax, and estate planning.

The book contains real-world examples, case studies, and professional insights that will deepen your comprehension and motivate you to take action.

1 — The Canadian Advantage

An Overview of the Canadian Real Estate Market

The Canadian real estate market is known for its resilience and stability. However, it is critical to note that the market varies significantly between regions and cities. When considering investing in the Canadian real estate market, keep the following aspects in mind:

1. *Market Cycles*

The Canadian real estate industry experiences expansion and recession like any other sector. You need to understand these cycles to make sound investment decisions. Critical evaluation of economic metrics, market dynamics, and historical data can help you determine the cycle's phase and predict future market trends.

For instance, when the economy is growing positively and interest rates have dropped, demand in the real estate sector usually rises, which generally results in high prices. On the contrary, during recessions or high interest rates, the market tends to experience slow growth, resulting in reduced property values.

2. *Regional Variations*

Canada is a large country with several distinct regions, each identified with unique economic factors and real estate dynamics. Cities and provinces may have different population growth rates, market demand, infrastructure development, and employment opportunities. You need to conduct an analysis and study to determine if you intend to find high investment prospects.

For instance, cities like Vancouver and Toronto have usually experienced high demand and rapid expansion; however, upcoming regions such as Calgary and Ottawa offer unique opportunities for investment due to regionally specific economic factors.

3 Market Policies and Regulations

Various policies and regulations govern the Canadian real estate industry at the local, provincial, and regional levels. These limitations may influence rental market laws, financing, taxation, zoning, and foreign investment. Always follow up on the current laws affecting the real estate industry to get a clear picture of the market and the risks linked to investments.

For example, recent policy adjustments, such as tighter mortgage stress tests or foreign buyer taxes in specific markets, influence market dynamics and impact property affordability.

Why Invest in the Canadian Real Estate?

Several advantages associated with the Canadian real estate industry make it domestically and internationally lucrative. Here are some benefits to consider:

1. *Security and Stability*

The Canadian real estate sector is known for its security and stability. It has stood the test of time, even during global economic recessions. Canada also has a solid legal framework, a stable political system, and straightforward property laws that make it a safe real estate investment haven.

For instance, during the global financial crisis of 2008, the Canadian real estate market was not significantly affected compared to other countries, courtesy of the strong mortgage laws and prudent lending culture.

2. *A Wide Pool of Investment Options*

A wide range of houses in Canada match various investment choices and risk tolerance. Investors have options, including industrial properties, commercial properties, multi-unit properties, and single-family homes. The variety enables investors to develop a complete portfolio that aligns with their financial goals.

For instance, residential properties may generate consistent rental income and witness value appreciation, while commercial assets may yield higher yields and longer lease terms.

3. Booming Rental Market

Canada boasts a booming rental market, which enables investors to generate steady income and accumulate capital. The market is catalyzed by factors such as population growth, urbanization, immigration, and first-time homebuyers' concerns regarding affordability. Renting properties offers tax advantages and creates a stable income source.

For example, cities with colleges and universities often experience a high demand for student rental properties, creating a steady stream of tenants.

Despite the many advantages associated with the Canadian real estate market, it is prudent to understand the accompanying risks. It is essential to apply proactive measures to overcome these limitations and enhance the chances of success. Below are some challenges to expect:

Budgetary Restrictions

Real estate is less inexpensive in Canadian regions and huge cities, where price hikes have been evident. Even so, there are solutions to affordability challenges, such as looking for alternative types of property that may attract better value or looking for emerging regions.

1. Mortgage and Financing Requirements

Securing mortgage financing can be challenging, especially for individuals with bad credit or first-time homebuyers. Therefore, it is essential to maintain a good credit score, develop a solid financial profile, and explore additional avenues of financing, such as collaborating with specialized lenders and partnering with other investors. These actions help eliminate the barriers of traditional funding.

2. *Competition and Market Volatility*

Market volatility can affect investment opportunities, especially in markets with high demand. To find an investment that fits your needs, it's essential to exercise patience, do thorough research, and focus on the market trends. Additionally, establishing connections with local real estate agents and industry specialists can yield valuable insights and access to off-market solutions.

One secret to finding potential deals before they are listed is to build positive relationships with real estate brokers, property managers, and local investors.

Always do extensive due diligence, consult industry experts, and never embrace continuous learning to help you make wise investment decisions.

2 — Establishing a Solid Foundation

Mindset Shift

A mindset shift matching financial success is the first step in developing a solid real estate investment.

First, you must embrace financial education and differentiate between liabilities and assets. Take a moment to think about your attitude toward wealth and money. Do you put more effort into acquiring liabilities that sweep away your money, such as heavy consumer debt or cars? Or do you focus more on acquiring income-generating assets to enhance your wealth creation efforts, such as business ventures and properties?

Invest your time in expanding your financial knowledge. You can do this by consulting real estate experts, attending seminars, and reading personal finance books. Being informed will empower you to navigate the real estate market and make sound decisions confidently.

Enhancing Financial Literacy

Adequate financial literacy is essential for successful real estate investing. First, you must master the financial concepts and refine your financial management skills. Below are some critical components of financial literacy:

Mastering Cash Flow

Cash flow is a critical component of real estate investment. It refers to the money that comes in and goes out of your real estate venture. When your rental income exceeds your expenses, we call it positive cash flow. When expenses are more than income, that's called negative cash flow. To maintain a positive cash flow, you have to generate income over time.

Let's say you buy a rental property worth $200,000. You generate a monthly revenue of $2,500 less expenses like mortgage payments, property taxes, maintenance fees, and insurance. If your monthly expenses total $2,000, you register a positive cash flow of $500.

Debt Management

Debt is an essential tool when used correctly. There are many types of debts, such as leverage and mortgages, and you can benefit from them as a real estate investor. You also need to understand the distinction between bad debt and good debt. Bad debt will siphon your finances, while good debt allows you to purchase income-generating assets.

When you obtain a mortgage, you use other people's finances to acquire real estate. You may then invest strategically, generate positive cash flow, and later utilize the rental income to repay the mortgage as you grow equity in your property.

Investment Opportunities Analysis

Another recipe for success in real estate investment is the prowess in analyzing investment prospects. You can do this by considering future growth potential, market demand, location, rental potential, and property condition. This analysis allows you to make intelligent decisions and identify profitable ventures.

These factors, which include rental demand, employment hubs, transport connections, and accessibility to amenities, must be considered during residential property analysis.

Building a Team

Teamwork is very essential in real estate investing. You should connect with a network of professionals who can guide your journey. These professionals may include property managers, real estate brokers, contractors, accountants, etc. You will need these professionals at one point in your real estate journey.

A local real estate agent can help you find ideal investment properties and receive crucial insights. You may also contact a property manager to handle day-to-day responsibilities such as upkeep and tenant management, allowing you to save time and manage your portfolio efficiently.

Goal Setting

You need to develop clear and realistic financial goals that will enable you to lay a strong foundation in your real estate investing. The following are steps you need to follow in setting clear and actionable goals:

1. **Define Your Vision**

Start by assessing your financial future and consider that your foundation. What does success mean to you? What matters to you the most: economic independence, early retirement, or a lasting legacy? A clear vision will enhance your focus and motivate you throughout your real estate investment journey.

Your goal may be to produce enough passive income from real estate investments to replace your existing income and attain financial independence.

2. **Set Specific Goals**

Set SMART (specific, measurable, attainable, relevant, and time-bound) goals to turn your vision into reality. You wish to make $5,000 in monthly revenue by purchasing three rental properties over the following two years. Specific goals will help you develop a plan to maintain motivation even as you monitor your progress.

3. **Take Massive Action**

Commit yourself to exceeding expectations. You could seek mentorship, pursue regular education, network with renowned professionals, or attend real estate events.

For instance, if you plan to acquire three rental properties, you may have to actively shop for investment alternatives, assess possible offers, and arrange financing to achieve your goals.

4. **Review and Adjust**

Conduct regular assessments of how you are progressing toward your goals. If there is a need, make adjustments, but remember that both the real estate industry and your individual might change. Therefore, you need to be flexible to keep your momentum and focus.

3— An Overview Canadian Real Estate Market

Research Market Demographics and Trends

One of the means to succeed in the Canadian real estate industry is to keep abreast of the demographics and market dynamics.

1. Market Trends Analysis

Since the Canadian real estate market is diverse, proper market trends analysis is essential to identify development potential in different regions. You can examine factors like industrial diversification, population growth, infrastructure development, and employment rates.

2. Demographic Considerations

Demographics is a very crucial factor to consider in real estate. Knowledge of demography composition is essential in predicting market stability and rent demand. Look for regions with favorable age demography, an increasing population, and solid economic indicators.

Demographic patterns can significantly enhance investment prospects. Areas with a growing population of young professionals may present a high demand for rental properties.

3. Researching Local Amenities

When evaluating potential investment properties, you should consider the availability of amenities. Facilities such as public transportation, retail centers, and green spaces usually attract renters and increase property value over time.

So, you need to find out the amenities available in the neighborhood. You can look for regions with many facilities that match different demographics and lifestyles. Such factors will make your property appealing to many potential tenants.

Mortgage Options and Financing Strategies

You need adequate knowledge of financing strategies and mortgage options to succeed in your real estate investment journey.

Saving for a Down Payment

The most critical first step in purchasing investment property is to set aside cash for a down payment. Set realistic savings targets and find strategies to multiply your savings. You can enhance your savings potential by sticking to a modest lifestyle and focusing more on increasing your income.

As an investor, you can explore alternative financing sources such as private equity, joint ventures, or partnerships. These strategies can help you overcome financial barriers and acquire investment properties soon.

Mortgage Pre-Approval

Start by obtaining a mortgage pre-approval from a reliable lender. This process includes sharing your financial details and finding out the approximate amount of loan you can borrow. Pre-approval enables you to understand your budget better and strengthens your buyer credibility.

Mortgage Options

Learn about the different types of mortgages in Canada to enable you to make intelligent choices, especially when financing your investment properties. Take into account variable-rate mortgages, adjustable-rate mortgages, and fixed-rate mortgages. Each one of these options has its advantages and disadvantages.

Investigating several lenders and mortgage programs is essential to determine which best aligns with your investing plan. For further guidelines, consult experienced mortgage experts. They might assist you in securing favorable mortgage terms and conditions.

Assessing Financing Strategies

Aside from conventional financing options, investors can choose from a pool of innovative financing alternatives. These strategies can diversify your real estate ventures and enhance your purchasing power.

You can finance your real estate investments using your RRSP (Registered Retirement Savings Plan), which allows you to enjoy the tax benefits of RRSP.

Partnerships and joint ventures are also another excellent option. Blending your experience and resources can help you reap the benefits of investing opportunities. For these tactics to succeed, there must be robust networking and a high level of trust.

Due Diligence and Risk Management

As a real estate investor, you should practice high levels of risk management and due diligence. Some components of due diligence and risk management include:

Creating a Contingency Fund

Having a contingency fund in place is essential, especially when handling unexpected expenses that may surface. You should set aside a portion of your rental income for this purpose. A contingency fund acts as a safety net by helping you handle unforeseen occurrences without negatively impacting your investment.

Set aside an amount that you can spend to handle unexpected events for three to six months.

Property Inspections

Conduct property inspections before you conclude the purchase process. Hire certified home inspectors to determine the property's condition, note potential issues, and calculate repair expenses. This stage enables you to bargain for competitive costs and make wise decisions.

Conduct a thorough evaluation and obtain as many quotes as possible for an accurate projection of remodeling expenses. This will ensure that the property matches your financial objectives while you save some cash.

Financial and Legal Due Diligence

Hire legal and financial due diligence professionals, such as real estate attorneys and accountants. To guarantee transparency and spot possible financial and legal issues, you might involve them in reviewing title documents, leases, financial records, and contracts.

Seek legal counsel before entering any contracts or committing yourself to any deal. By understanding fully the legal ramifications of your investments, you can reduce risks and secure your financial interests.

Assessing Rental Potential

Assessing a property's rental potential can help determine whether it will attract income. Check the region's rental rates, vacancy rates, and rental demand.

Having a rough idea of the area's tenant preferences can enable you to conduct market research to analyze the rental prospects. This data is essential in determining your expected rental income before deciding.

4— Taking Advantage of Leverage

Proper Utilization of Finances

Finance is like the engine of your real estate investing journey and can significantly impact your success. Therefore, financing options are essential to accelerate wealth building and eventually gain higher returns.

In reference to real estate, leverage can be defined as a calculative usage of borrowed cash to finance real estate ventures. Instead of paying cash, you can get a mortgage and make a small down payment. By doing this, you utilize a portion of the capital to take complete control of the property's value.

Assume you find a property valued at $500,000 property. You can make a down payment of $100,000 and acquire a loan-to-value mortgage of 80% for the other $400,000. Your return on investment (ROI) comprises the 5% return on your initial $100,000 investment and a 25% return on the $500,000 overall value if the property appreciates by 5% within a year.

This strategy aligns with what prominent real estate investors implement: leveraging leverage. You can enhance your cash flow and holdings by considering conducive financing options and favorable interest rates. The main goal is to reap good cash flow from rental income.

Before utilizing any debt, you should start by determining the Return on Investment (ROI). ROI is your approximate investment profit, accounting for real estate appreciation and cash flow.

ROI is calculated by considering the property's net operating income (NOI), which represents the total rental income, and subtracting operating expenses. The NOI is then divided by the initial investment, including the down payment and closing fees.

This will yield a percentage that represents the return on investment. Additionally, consider the potential for property gains over time, as this increases the return on investment overall.

For instance, you purchase an investment property worth $300,000. After subtracting operational costs, including property taxes, maintenance, and management fees, the property earns a net operating income of $30,000 annually. Your total investment will be $70,000 after paying $10,000 in closing charges and a $60,000 down payment. The ROI is approximately 42.9% when the $30,000 NOI is divided by the $70,000 investment.

Taking full charge of the debt-to-income ratio when utilizing leverage is essential. Lenders use this ratio to determine whether an investor can repay loans. A lower debt-to-income ratio indicates a positive financial standing, enabling you to secure better financial deals.

The debt-income ratio is determined by dividing your overall monthly debt commitments, such as credit card payments, mortgage payments, and other loans, by your gross monthly income. Lenders usually prefer a debt-to-income ratio that is below 43%.

Mortgage Strategies

A more profound knowledge of mortgage strategies can help you get the highest investment returns.

The most common method of financing real estate is traditional mortgages. You can contribute at least 20% of the property's purchase price as a down payment, cut costly mortgage insurance fees, and benefit from favorable interest rates. This type of mortgage works well for a buy-and-hold approach in the long run.

Let's say you want to acquire a house worth $400,000. Usually, you will need to make a down payment of not less than 20%, which will be $80,000. You will then acquire a mortgage to fund the remaining balance of $320,000. When you put down a more significant amount, you reduce the loan-to-value (LTV) ratio and reduce your mortgage amount, leading to reduced interest rates and lower monthly payments.

You can also acquire a house even if you have less than 20% of the property's value as a down payment, but in this case, through high-ratio mortgages. Whereas a mortgage is needed to act as security for lenders, these mortgages permit lenders to include more capital in other assets, leveraging the property's cash flow.

Let's say you want to acquire a home worth $300,000 but can only afford a down payment of $30,000. You can utilize a high-ratio mortgage to finance the balance of $270,000. Remember that the overall cost of high-ratio mortgages includes mortgage insurance. This option may still be viable, provided that your property's cash flow can cater to insurance expenses and mortgage payments.

During favorable circumstances, you can pursue mortgage refinancing. Cutting your monthly mortgage payments can free up your money for additional investments. You can also get equity to finance property upgrades by substituting your current mortgage with a new one.

For instance, if you own a property whose value has appreciated since you purchased it, you can utilize the equity built into the property for various purposes through refinancing. You can use the proceeds to acquire or facelift another home to raise its value. You should consider the potential benefits and costs of refinancing, including interest rates, closing expenses, and the effect on overall financial standing.

Using Other People's Money to Build Wealth

Using other people's money, also known as OPM, is a strategy for leveraging other people's finances to enhance one's capacity for investing.

To secure more profitable and ambitious real estate ventures, investors pool their talents, knowledge, and resources through joint ventures and partnerships. Collaboration allows investors to access initiatives and resources that would have otherwise been difficult to access.

For example, if you find a business property with potential for good income and don't have ready money to acquire and renovate it as an individual. In that case, you can enter a partnership or joint venture with other investors, bring your resources together, and divide the costs. This partnership enhances purchasing power, brings more experience, and spreads risks.

You can also explore other financing sources like syndication and private lenders. Private lenders are companies or individuals who lend cash to investors and get the money back with interest. Syndication is the process of gathering funds from different investors to fund massive projects.

Private lenders play a significant role, especially when securing regular funding is challenging or when an investor requires flexible terms. Private lenders typically follow various criteria and are ready to lend finances depending on the investor's track record or the potential of a property. Collaborating with private lenders can help you get money for short-term needs, improvements, or property purchases.

Syndication pools funds together, thereby allowing investors to access significant investment opportunities. These collaborations can enable you to participate in projects above your financial muscles. Syndication comes in different forms, including real estate investment trusts (REITs) and limited partnerships. This can also help you diversify your portfolio and expose you to various property types and markets.

For instance, investors might pool their finances to acquire a multi-unit residential property. The partial contributions from each investor offer adequate purchasing power to buy the property. Here, each investor shares a portion of rewards and risks proportional to the amount each one contributed. Consequently, individual investors can participate in larger-scale programs and take advantage of the group's resources and experience.

One strategy that real estate investors are employing to access OPM is crowdfunding. These networks link projects that require funding with people willing to invest. This allows individuals who want to invest but need more money to take part in real estate investment with what they have.

Crowdfunding initiatives allow both non-accredited and accredited real estate investors to participate in transactions. These initiatives provide various options with diverse risk profiles and projected income, and they usually perform in-depth due diligence. Through this, you can explore potential projects, assess detailed project specifics, and make knowledge-based decisions.

Let's say you find a crowdsourcing website with an opportunity to contribute to constructing a new house. Depending on your risk tolerance and investment goals, you can assess the project details, such as expected returns, financial estimates, development history, and location, and then decide how much you will pump in. This is an excellent opportunity to diversify your real estate holdings using minimum financial investments or with minimum knowledge in specific fields.

Employing smart financial tactics, having the correct information about mortgage options, and cleverly utilizing other people's money can accelerate your wealth-building rate.

Remember to seek professional guidance from experts such as real estate gurus, mortgage brokers, accountants, etc., to help you understand financing options that can apply to your individual situation.

5— Financing Options

There is a wide range of financing options you can opt for when you want to dive into the Canadian real estate industry. Let's explore some of these options.

Traditional Mortgage Financing

Conventional mortgage financing is one of the most prevalent strategies real estate investors employ. It entails borrowing money from a financial entity, such as a bank or credit union, to pay for the purchase of a home. This is how it works:

1. *Down Payment*

One requirement for applying for a traditional mortgage to acquire a property is to offer a down payment, which is a percentage of the home's buying price. The down payment depends on the acquisition cost and the type of property.

2. *Loan Terms*

Traditional mortgages offer a range of loan terms, such as variable or fixed interest rates and loan periods of 15 to 30 years. You should carefully read the terms and choose an option that matches your financial capability.

3. *Qualification Requirements*

Financial institutions consider factors like the consistency of your income, creditworthiness, and debt-to-income ratio to determine your eligibility for a mortgage. They also assess your financial status to determine the maximum amount of loan you qualify for.

4. Interest Rates

Traditional mortgages usually have fixed or variable interest rates. The fixed rate doesn't change for the entire mortgage duration, offering monthly predictability and consistency. On the other hand, variable rates change depending on market dynamics, which may lead to cost increases or decreases.

5. Amortization

Amortization refers to paying back your mortgage in installments over time. Extended amortization periods typically attract lower monthly payments but higher overall interest costs.

Home Equity Line of Credit (HELOC)

A Home Equity Line of Credit (HELOC) is an additional financing alternative Canadians can access to fund their real estate investments. Here is how it operates:

- **Equity Utilization**

You can utilize a home equity loan (HELOC) as collateral to access the equity accumulated in your existing property. It offers a credit line that is accessible at any time, up to a certain amount.

- **Flexibility**

One significant advantage of HELOCs is that they are very flexible. You are only required to pay interest on the amount you borrow, enabling you to borrow as much as you require. This flexibility is advantageous, especially to people who need instant access to capital for repairs or improvements to their properties.

- **Interest Rates**

Variable interest rates on HELOCs are typically correlated with a benchmark rate, like the prime rate. Therefore, you should consider thoroughly the impact of interest changes on your borrowing expenses.

- **Repayment Options**

You might be required to make interest-only payments for the draw term period, usually a few years. Upon the conclusion of the draw period, you might need to turn the balance into a traditional mortgage.

HELOCs enable real estate investors to access their funds flexibly and are a valuable tool for acquiring home equity for various purposes. However, you need to utilize this financing option cautiously and consider the risks and costs involved.

Private Financing

Private financing refers to acquiring finances from private lending companies or private individuals instead of conventional institutions. Here is what you need to know before opting for private funding:

- **Networks and Relationships:** To find potential private lenders, you need to build networks and personal connections. Building relationships with private lenders can provide you access to flexible financing.

- **Negotiable Terms:** Private financing is more flexible regarding collateral requirements, repayment schedules, and interest rates. However, you need to assess whether the requirements are acceptable and reasonable.

- **Higher Interest Rates:** Since private financing exposes lenders to more risk, it usually comes with higher interest rates than traditional mortgages. Nonetheless, when conventional financing options are limited, private financing can provide funds instantly.

Private financing is a better option for individuals who are unqualified for traditional mortgages or need funds urgently for opportunities that involve investments that should be made before the deadline. Therefore, you should maintain constant communication and establish trust with private lenders to create mutual partnerships.

Taking Advantage of Government Programs and Incentives

The Canadian government provides several programs and incentives to assist real estate investors. These programs increase investment, encourage affordable housing, and make homeownership more accessible.

Some examples of these programs include:

1. Canada Mortgage and Housing Corporation (CMHC) Programs

CMHC offers financial aid to qualified developers and individuals with programs like the Rental Construction Financing Initiative and First-Time Home Buyer Incentive. These programs provide real estate investors with capital and incentives and enable them to achieve their investment goals.

2. Municipal and Provincial Programs

Most provinces and municipalities have their own programs to encourage real estate investment, such as development subsidies, tax incentives, and affordable housing. These programs vary depending on the region. Therefore, you need to familiarize yourself with the programs in the area where you intend to invest.

3. **Registered Retirement Savings Plan (RRSP) Home Buyers' Plan**

RRSP Home Buyers' Plan enables homebuyers to withdraw a certain amount from their RRSPs without being penalized. This is a beneficial initiative for real estate investors since it may be utilized to fund a down payment on a property.

Government incentives and initiatives can offer real estate investors more financial aid and property development opportunities. Conduct a thorough assessment to understand eligibility requirements, obligations attached to these initiatives, and the application process.

Creative Financing Strategies

In addition to government initiatives and traditional financing tactics, investors can use other creative financing alternatives to enhance their real estate ventures.

These strategies may include:

1. **Vendor Take-Back Mortgage:** Under this strategy, the property seller becomes the financer and lends the buyer money to acquire the property. This approach applies mainly when traditional financing alternatives are limited and the seller is keen to close a purchase.

2. **Partnerships and Joint Ventures:** As stated earlier in this book, investors can come together to pool more resources and funds. These collaborations can be established in various ways and help broaden your real estate ventures or investigate more ambitious projects.

3. **Creative Lease Options:** As an investor, you can lease a property with an option to purchase it at a fixed price within a certain period. If you want to maintain control over a property but are not prepared to assume ownership instantly, it might be helpful to try this strategy. Through this strategy, you can generate money, assess the property's potential, and decide if exercising your purchase option is worthwhile in the long run.

4. **Seller Financing:** In seller financing, the person selling the property gives the buyer funds in the form of a second mortgage. This strategy is beneficial, especially when traditional lenders seem more reluctant to offer the whole financial amount or when the seller wants to speed up the sale process. You can negotiate favorable terms for seller financing, such as reduced interest rates or adjustable repayment periods.

These creative financial options present new avenues for investors to broaden their investment, acquire capital, or arrange real estate deals.

6 — Building Your Real Estate Portfolio

Setting Investment Goals

You must set clear goals to take your real estate investment to the next level. Clear goals are a roadmap to your financial journey and ensure you don't divert attention. Below are some elements you need to take into account once you are ready to invest:

1. *Financial Goals*

Be specific on your financial goals, such as monthly cash flow, annual ROI, or monthly cash flow. Create realistic goals to track your progress and assess your portfolio's performance.

2. *Time Horizon*

To determine your investment time horizon, consider your risk tolerance, age, and estimated retirement age. Shorter investment horizons should be exercised with great caution. However, longer horizons encourage more aggressive development strategies.

3. *Risk Appetite*

Before implementing any investment strategy, assess your risk tolerance and comfort level. Building a portfolio entails taking various levels of risk as well as being familiar with your risk tolerance to select suitable investments.

4. *Exit Strategy*

Ensure each investment in your portfolio consists of an exit strategy. Settle on the best method and time for selling your assets to rebalance your portfolio or optimize earnings. A well-designed exit strategy prepares you for any market dynamics and shifts in the circumstances around your investments.

Clear investment goals allow you to establish and manage your real estate portfolio using a calculated and targeted approach.

Capitalization and Financing

You need additional capital and financing to expand your real estate ventures. Here are some things to keep in mind:

- **Access to Capital:** Assess your financial resources and consider additional options such as traditional mortgages, lines of credit, private financing, and joint ventures. You can get the money you need to expand your portfolio by evaluating your financial situation and looking into creative financing options.

- **Cash Flow Management:** Cash flow management becomes even more essential as you acquire additional properties. When examining your ability to expand your investment, consider your current income, potential vacancies, and projected costs. Implement effective cash flow management to ensure a financially stable portfolio.

- **Equity and Leverage:** Utilize the equity in your current properties to fund additional acquisitions. You can leverage the increasing value of your properties and use the extra money to expand your portfolio by using home equity lines of credit (HELOCs) or refinancing.

Establishing a Diversified Real Estate Portfolio

Having a diversified real estate portfolio enables you to boost returns and lower risks. By spreading your investments over various geographic regions, markets, and property types. Spreading your investments over various property kinds, markets, and geographic areas results in diversification. The following approaches can help you create a diversified portfolio:

1. *Property Types*

To diversify, you can consider investing in different property types. The risk profiles and market dynamics of multifamily, residential, commercial, retail, and industrial assets vary. Diversifying your property portfolio of properties can mitigate the impacts of specific market conditions or fluctuations in the industry.

For example, if you own residential and commercial office properties, you can have a properly balanced portfolio that is unshaken by the dynamics of either sector.

2. *Geographic Locations*

Acquiring property across various regions may help safeguard your portfolio against regional market dynamics. Regional variations regarding economic conditions, population growth, and employment rates are essential. Establishing investments across several cities or regions can enable you to take advantage of opportunities in rapidly expanding markets and minimize vulnerability to market dynamics.

3. *Market Segments*

To diversify your wealth, invest in multiple real estate market niches. Consider retail assets, residential rents, industrial warehouses, and commercial office space. Since different sectors may have other risk considerations and demand drivers, diversifying among them will allow you to balance your portfolio.

Consider varying your portfolio with every market segment in terms of your property's price range, quality, and size. Doing this reduces the risk of overspending on a tenant or single property while appealing to a diverse pool of potential tenants.

Managing and Optimizing Your Portfolio

To achieve long-term success in real estate, you need to optimize and manage your portfolio efficiently. The following are some critical concepts to manage and optimize your portfolio:

- **Professional Property Management**

Consider hiring expert property management services to manage the day-to-day operations of your assets. Property managers can help you handle general administrative duties, property upkeep, rent collection, and tenant screening. You can relieve yourself of these duties and focus on expanding your portfolio and making strategic decisions.

- **Performance Monitoring and Analysis**

Monitor the performance of your property regularly and pay attention to key performance indicators to identify areas that require optimization and enhancement. Here are essential metrics you should consider:

Cash Flow:

Asses the cash flow of each property, taking into consideration both rental income and expenses. Identify the properties with a solid cash flow and those requiring adjustments to enhance profitability.

Return on Investment (ROI):

Calculate the ROI for each property by considering the asset appreciation, rental income, financing charges, and the purchase price. Examine the return on your investments and find strategies to enhance them.

Occupancy Rates:

Examine the occupancy rates and note any challenges or trends that can impact rental income. Respond to openings regularly and implement market campaigns that attract and retain qualified renters.

Market Trends:

Stay updated on changes in market movements, economic data, and regulations that may impact your portfolio. Also, stay informed about any news about neighborhood development plans, interest rates, and rental situations to make intelligent decisions concerning your property.

7— Optimizing Your Cash Flow

Implementing Efficient Property Management Techniques

You must utilize efficient estate management approaches to maximize the income flow of your real estate ventures. These approaches ensure that your properties are well taken care of. Let's consider some strategies you can implement to enhance your income flow.

Screening and Selecting Quality Tenants

Managing an investment entails selecting reliable and conscientious tenants. Conduct an in-depth screening to assess potential tenants. This could involve assessing their credit history, confirming their income and employment, contacting past tenants for references, and conducting background checks. Finding quality tenants can significantly enhance your cash flow by minimizing the possibility of property damage, evictions, and late payment.

Strategic Rental Pricing

Finding the right rental price is essential to boosting revenue flow. Conduct an in-depth market analysis to determine rental charges in your area. Consider the size, state, amenities, and location of your property. Come up with a competitive rental price that will attract a good return on investment and appeal to renters.

For instance, if you own properties in the downtown area of Toronto, find out the rental price in the nearby properties. If your property has extra facilities or amenities, you can charge more for the rental price.

Efficient Rent Collection

Using simple rent collection methods is critical to maintaining a steady flow of income. Effective rent collection strategies include online payment portals or automated bank transfers. Make your expectations clear regarding rent due dates and penalties for late payment.

Proactive Property Maintenance

Regular property maintenance is critical to keep its value and attract high-quality tenants. Incorporate sporadic fixes, routine inspections, and preventive maintenance processes. Respond immediately to maintenance requests to prevent significant issues that might attract huge repair expenses from occurring.

Streamlining Operational Efficiency

You should conduct effective operational management to optimize cash flow operations. You can increase profitability in your real estate holdings by optimizing procedures and reducing expenses. Now let us highlight some approaches to enhance operational effectiveness:

- **Cost Optimization**

Assess your operating costs and find areas where you can cut expenses without negatively impacting the quality of your property or tenant satisfaction. You should negotiate directly with service providers and suppliers to get better prices. Consider buying supplies in large quantities to get better discounts and save some cash. Examine your expenses regularly to find areas where you might save some funds.

- **Energy Efficiency**

Use energy-efficient solutions in your houses to reduce utility expenses and attract mindful renters. You can install LED lighting, add more insulation, or replace old gadgets with energy-efficient ones. Give your tenants instructional materials and incentivize them to encourage them to use energy-saving solutions.

- **Technology and Automation**

Adopt the use of technology in administrative tasks, record-keeping, and communication. Utilize property management systems to automate rent collection, lease renewals, and maintenance requests. Use internet apps or portals to enhance communication between tenants and property managers. Employing technology and automation minimizes errors, saves time, and increases effectiveness.

Minimizing Tenant Turnover and Vacancy

Minimizing vacancies and tenant turnover is essential to ensure a steady cash flow. The following strategies can help you achieve this:

1. **Tenant Retention**

Focus on tenant satisfaction and maintain an atmosphere that encourages long-term tenancy. Build a culture of responding to tenants' concerns and requests quickly. Stay in constant communication with renters to build a strong relationship with them. You can also offer incentives to renters to encourage them to stay.

For example, if a tenant takes good care of the facilities and pays rent on time, you can show them gratitude by slightly reducing their rent.

2. **Effective Marketing and Advertising**

Implement effective marketing techniques to attract qualified renters and minimize vacancies. You can promote your rental properties using online listing services, local magazines, and social media. Attract prospective tenants by sharing the unique attributes of your property, amenities, and location benefits. Capitalize on prospective clients by responding to their inquiries promptly and arranging property viewings.

Create attractive internet listings with straightforward descriptions and high-quality photos. Emphasize each property's benefits and unique selling points to attract potential tenants.

3. Lease Renewal Planning

Be proactive during lease renewals and inform the tenants before their lease expires. During lease renewal, recognize their goals and negotiate the terms earlier. Early lease renewals can help you mitigate vacant periods and guarantee steady cash flow.

For example, as a landlord, you can contact your tenants three to six months before lease expiry to learn about their plans and work on the renewal terms. This allows you to budget ahead of time and adjust your cash flow projections.

8— Legacy Planning and Long-Term Wealth

Preserving Wealth through Real Estate

If done strategically, real estate can be a great place to preserve wealth. As an investor, you need to take proactive steps to protect your investments and financial stability. Here are a few ways real estate can preserve your wealth:

1. **Asset Protection**

One tactic to safeguard your wealth through real estate is utilizing legal frameworks for asset protection. Find an experienced lawyer or other professional legal services to help you identify ideal entities to store your real estate investments. Limited liability companies (LLCs), trusts, and corporations offer varied levels of security against possible personal liability and litigation.

For example, if you win several investment properties, you can establish separate LLCs for each to isolate and protect them from any risks that may arise.

2. **Insurance Coverage**

Comprehensive insurance coverage is essential to minimize risks of unforeseen disasters, liability claims, and property damage. Contact an insurance professional to determine the suitable coverage for your properties. Check whether your insurance coverage adequately safeguards and provides liability to your assets.

For example, you might need additional coverage, such as business interruption and liability insurance, to protect yourself from third parties and tenant lawsuits.

3. **Regular Property Evaluations**

Assess the performance and value of your real estate assets regularly. Stay updated with changes in local regulations, the state of your property, and market trends. Find out what needs maintenance, and check any opportunities for repairs and upgrades that could raise the value of your property and increase your rental income.

Keeping a close eye on your portfolio and being proactive can enable you to identify any areas of improvement or possible risks so you can move swiftly to protect your investment.

Tax Strategies for Canadian Real Estate Investors

Finding the proper tax mechanisms helps improve your real estate holdings and optimize your long-term wealth. You can consider the following tax planning strategies:

a. Capital Gains Tax Planning

When selling a property, know the consequences of tax gains. Consult a tax professional to help you establish a plan for tracking your capital gains tax liability. You employ strategies such as structuring transactions to minimize taxable gains, taking advantage of the principle home exemption, or delaying capital gains via a like-kind change exchange (Section 1031 exchange).

For instance, if you wish to sell a property that is your primary residence, ensure you comply with the requirements to qualify for the principal residence exemption. That will enable you to minimize or altogether avoid capital gains tax.

b. Deductible Expenses

Find out how to optimize the deductible expenses linked to your real estate investments. Seek advice from a tax expert or accountant familiar with real estate taxation to ensure you optimize all potential deductions. Some examples of typical deductibles include professional charges, property tax, maintenance and repair, mortgage interest, and property management costs.

c. Incorporation Strategies

Consider incorporating your real estate holdings to increase your portfolio management flexibility and save on taxes. Speak with a tax expert or accountant to determine if incorporation suits your situation and investment goals. Some benefits of incorporation may be enhanced asset protection, income splitting, and access to corporate tax rates.

Wealth Transfer and Estate Planning

Planning for wealth transfer to future generations is critical in long-term financial strategy. By planning carefully, you can achieve seamless transfer and preserve your legacy. Real estate can contribute to enhancing your estate planning. Keep the following components of estate planning in mind:

1. Trusts and Wills

You can seek the services of an estate planning lawyer to help you draft a detailed will specifying your wishes concerning the distribution of your real estate assets. You can establish a trust since it can help you manage and preserve your real estate investments and offer your heirs significant tax advantages, privacy, and freedom.

For instance, to secure the management and transfer of your property to your beneficiaries, you can set up a testamentary trust via your will, and upon your death, it will be activated.

2. Succession Planning

Succession planning is essential to ensure a seamless transfer of management and ownership. Consider enlisting the support of reliable advisers, key staff members, and close relatives to support decision-making and management. Write your succession plan and share it with all key stakeholders to ensure clarity and eliminate possible disputes.

For example, if your children wish to continue in real estate investing, establish a clear plan outlining their obligations and the process for transitioning management authority and ownership.

3. Charitable Giving

Consider including charitable giving in your plan to support projects dear to you and may receive tax benefits. Consult an estate planning expert to help you decide which option to include in your will between charitable bequests, charity trust creation, and foundation creation.

For example, you may donate a real estate asset to a nonprofit to support the cause and receive tax benefits, such as a charitable deductions.

Conclusion

In conclusion, while the Canadian real estate industry is full of opportunities, it also has a distinct set of challenges. When making investment decisions, you should conduct thorough research, keep up with market developments, and consider economic indicators, financing possibilities, and location factors.

Furthermore, you can navigate the complexities of the Canadian real estate sector by working closely with reputable real estate experts and financial advisers. If you carefully analyze investments and consider the long-term view, you stand a chance to reap the growth potential and stability of the Canadian real estate market.

NOTES

www.ingramcontent.com/pod-product-compliance
Lightning Source LLC
Chambersburg PA
CBHW050318100526
44585CB00016BA/1729